Contents

What's a Greyhound book?

Greyhounds are quick, they're also not keen on big books.

Seriously though – sometimes you don't necessarily have the time to wade through a whole 350 page book. Sometimes you just want a bit of condensed entertainment.

Acknowledgements

Thanks to Tim, Penny and all at GRWE.

Thanks for all greyhound rescue charities everywhere for doing what you do.

Thankyou Abbie and Mr P for bumping into me when you did.

Thankyou Sean the Greyhound. Not least for our Twitter conversations. And also for your wonky run and inability to read.

Foreword

Thankyou for buying this book.

Fancy some life coaching on the cheap? Read on for the pearls of wisdom handed on to me by my rescued dog, Sean.

I didn't think I needed much help with running my life – least of all from a two-year-old greyhound who was considered too rubbish to race; a dog whose only experience of life was the boredom of long hours spent alone in a bare kennel, with occasional minutes of running around in circles; a dog who hadn't even been taught his own name. How wrong I was...It's been life-changing.

Sean and I have not known each other very long – but so far, it's been a blast.

Sean

Greyhounds get the roughest of rough deals. They have virtually no puppyhood, but go straight to being trained to race. If they don't make the grade, they generally are disposed of. Even the successful ones are usually ditched when they can no longer win. The very few fortunate ones are rehomed.

It was for this reason I decided that if I were ever to have a dog, I would rescue a greyhound. A chance encounter with an elderly gentleman and his greyhound, Abbie, sealed my fate.

After a few months' thinking time, my husband and I were vetted, and then paired with our potential hound. I say 'potential', I don't think there was any doubt – we were definitely going to take this furry, long-legged chap home.

Sean knew nothing when he arrived. He didn't even know his name.

He also was completely confused by stairs and why we felt the need to have any at all.

Our friends' children were puzzled when they offered him a treat and he wouldn't sit. 'He doesn't do 'sit',' we'd say.

In spite of being previously classed as the kennel idiot, once Sean settled into his new life he soon started picking things up. He is now very happy to do whatever is asked – as long as he knows what is expected.

Sean is a very valuable addition to our family, we don't know what we'd do without him. Buy a telly, probably. He provides us with entertainment every day – not least when he has a big stretch and a trump comes out by accident, making him jump. Seriously. How much fun?!

1

All things are possible.
Even stairs.

Stairs are tricky when you're tall and have four long legs. But there's always a challenge with anything that's really worth doing.

2

It's OK to be naked.

OK, this only counts if you're a dog. But then, if you were, why would you be reading this?

Be free. And recognise how good that feels.

3

Live in the present too.

Whilst it is important and responsible to plan for the future, it is also important to enjoy the present. That long walk with lots of things to sniff, if you're a greyhound, or perhaps that surprise afternoon off that gives time that can just be enjoyed, if you're not.

4

Don't skimp on sleep.

It's important, it's how your brain processes and repairs. It will leave you refreshed, if you've done it properly.

5

It's OK to obsess about things.

Greyhounds are often obsessed by food – a life with a purpose and a passion is a life well-lived.

6

Be optimistic.

As long as there's a light on in the kitchen, there's always a chance of a treat. Until there's no possibility, there's always a chance.

7

Walk closely with the one you love.

There's nothing like going through life with someone nice. Spend time giving them unconditional attention. Small gestures count.

8

It's quicker to learn if you take time to understand the point.

Sitting? Schmitting.

But all of a sudden it's a whole lot easier to learn something when one realises it's the key to getting all the finest treats.

9

It's OK to ignore people if they're not being specific.

There are plenty of people making noise in the world – but we don't need to take notice of all of them all of the time. Wait for some words that interest you. Like 'dinner' and 'walk'.

10

Master the art of walking quietly.

Sometimes there may be cats. Don't miss out on a good opportunity because you're too clumsy to grab it with both paws.

11

You're tired? It's OK to fall asleep in public.

It's a great use of time, and, chances are, people will think you're cute when you're snoring your head off.

12

Life is too short to have a walk with no bounce.

Keep your head up high. You're you – and you're better at being you than anyone else.

13

At a loose end? Find someone to give you a hug.

If it's not time for dinner, and it's not time for a walk, what's a dog to do?

Find someone to give you a hug, that's what. It'll make both of you feel good.

14

Not all cats are for catching.

Some things will pass you by. It's OK. Don't look back. Just move on.

15

It's the little dogs that yap the loudest.

And they don't necessarily have anything constructive to say. You don't need to give limitless airtime to prolonged yapping.

Sometimes people have a point. Sometimes they don't.

Be fair – but move on if you need to. No one needs to be yapped at.

16

Sitting nicely reaps rewards.

It's OK to sometimes do the expected thing. And doing it more often yields more frequent rewards.

17

It's OK to be dependent. No one thinks any less of you.

In today's society 'being a burden' is considered to be pretty much the worst thing you can do to your family. That's rubbish.

Families and their members will only thrive when they love and are loved, care and are cared for.

18

Yogurt pot lids are not worth bothering with. Wait for the actual pot to be handed over.

Don't get distracted by the little things. Focus on the main event, and go all-out.

19

A friend who waits patiently while you sniff things is truly a friend indeed.

True friends give you the time and space to be you, and appreciate what things you enjoy, even if they don't share the hobby.

20

Avoid the vacuum cleaner at all costs.

No explanation or clarification needed.

So what if no one has actually been sucked up yet?

It could still happen.

21

Pick your battles, and your cats, carefully.

Do what's definitely achievable first before moving onto more difficult tasks. Some things are for another day. Know the difference.

22

Looking dapper should be effortless.

If you can't give that waxed jacket a raffish air without trying, perhaps move to a less challenging wardrobe item such as an anorak.

23

A comfy bed is an essential indeed.

Comfort matters. There's no sense in pretending you're too cool for comfort.

24

The sofa is to be aspired to.

Aspirations are good. Try, try, try again, and then accept that some things are out of your reach.

25

If someone loves you,
they'll not mind your gas.

- Although they may try to alter your diet
to reduce the pungency.

26

Master the art of looking cute.

One is never too old for this sort of lark. Manage this and the world will be in your paws – and every spare crust will have your name on.

27

Be genuinely pleased to see people.

Check their pockets if necessary. But generally speaking, people are a Very Good Thing.

28

Make dinner an occasion.

One doesn't have many dinners in a day. Make each one count.

29

Be committed to your job.

Whatever your rule in life, whether it's keeping an eye on the kitchen or checking under furniture for crumbs, it's your job – so do it to the best of your ability. Be thorough. Be magnificent.

30

The ultimate prize is cheese.

Forsake all for this. A few things are seriously worth putting oneself out for.

31

Get up and out early.

The early bird catches the worm. And even if you don't want a worm, it's still good to be up early. Just think of the possibilities every day offers!

32

Make your own entertainment.

TV is overrated, however, the recycling box and its contents are fair game.

33

Talking of fair game, if it's in your reach, you can have it...

...Otherwise they would have moved it. Everything can be an opportunity for those who are alert to the possibilities.

34

Do your stretches regularly and frequently.

Otherwise, how will you maintain that wonderful, athletic and majestic physique?

35

Listen carefully to people.

It may sound like 'blah, blah, blah', but at some point someone's going to say something that matters. Like 'biscuit'. Or 'dinner'.

36

Don't trust other people with your dinner.

Eat quickly so on one can steal your biscuits. One never knows.

37

Clothes are boring presents.

Buy food or thoughtful items as gifts, not utilitarian things. A coat is dull.

38

Manners will ultimately get you what you want.

It's a pain to learn manners, but they're excellent tools for getting what you want in life.

39

A wag costs nothing.

Brighten someone's day. Just being you should do it.

40

What goes in most definitely must come out.

Carrier bags may seem fun at the time, but they're really not such a good idea. Appearances can be deceptive.

41

Dogs are from Mars, Swans are definitely from somewhere else.

No one knows where they're from, or exactly what they're for. Just stay out of the way.

42

Always have a strategy.

Food is good. Having one's ears played with is just OK, but be patient, and a treat may result as well.

43

It's OK to be good-looking.

It's even better to be good-looking and never give it a moment's thought.

44

Respect older dogs.

The older generation has seen, heard, and experienced a great deal more than you have. They weren't always grey-muzzled and slow, and they're likely to be more frustrated than you realise that movement doesn't come as easily. Be patient. Give time, space, and an encouraging wag.

45

Get up early on Sunday.

Prepare for a long and full day of relaxation.
Mmmmmm!

46

Chase a ball?

Some tasks will generate their own work. Recognise them for what they are and steer clear.

47

Barking. There's just no need.

Be calm, quiet and considered. People will appreciate it.

48

Show someone you love them by watching them eat.

Nothing says 'I love you' like a food stalker.

49

Be good-natured.

If you're the brunt of jokes, you must be very well-loved.

50

Pigeons are rubbish.

Some things can appear promising, only to disappear on closer inspection. Learn from it and move on. Don't dwell on the unfairness of life.

51

Being constantly on the go doesn't make you a better person.

It does, however, make you tired. Just give it a rest and chill.

52

It's OK to be keen.

But don't risk biting people's hands off. Even if it's for cheese.

53

Go out for regular breaks.

It's refreshing and it's good for concentration, productivity and relaxation.

54

Use time wisely.

If people have nothing interesting to say, you can still make use of the time spent at a dull dinner party by catching up on some sleep.

55

Life is sometimes cruel.

When you're told it's 'cheese' and it actually turns out to be 'bath', give yourself a shake and move on. Show others you're the better person in the situation. Go with the flow. (Ha ha.)

56

Always make your bed.

This is simply and quickly done by walking around in circles a few times on it. Perfect.

57

Every day is a school day.

Get streets ahead of every other pooch by learning as much English as possible. Humans will drop things in conversation thinking you won't understand. Many treats have been missed through lack of vigilance.

58

It's OK not to wear clothes in the house.

Just don't draw attention to yourself by scratching anything.

59

Teach the people around you how to have fun.

A great game is to teach humans the trick of opening a breadbin without waking you up. It's great fun – particularly if they don't mind losing!

60

Be enthusiastic.

Even looking more enthusiastic than you feel can reap tremendous rewards. Sometimes there are hidden treats that may be on offer to those who show the most enthusiasm.

61

Don't cause offence.

If you're going to stand on someone's feet, make sure you've had your toenails cut. And also, look as cute as possible.

62

Persistence pays.

Persistence and cuteness pays dividends. It's a fact.

63

If they love you, they'll clean up after you.

And if they love you lots, they won't even mention it.

64

Appreciate the little things.

A cosy bed is a blessing indeed.

65

Be resourceful.

One man's under-the-desk legroom is another dog's day bed.

66

Avoid futility

Running around in circles only benefits other people.

67

Everyone has a price.

Everyone has things that make them tick.
Even if it's just cheese.

68

You don't have to let sleeping dogs lie.

The current situation will perpetuate unless you're prepared to do something about it. Greyhounds won't mind if you wake them up – they're quite happy to curl up somewhere else and catch up on that mini-hibernation that happens every day, about this time.

69

'Nuff small talk. Get down to business.

Don't waste time discussing the weather, when actually there's something you need to get off your chest. Likewise, if that's a new acquaintance right there – head straight for the pockets; they may be bearing gifts.

70

Cultivate a masterful eyebrow.

Yes, dispense with needless commentary. An eyebrow expresses 1,000 words.

71

Don't worry.

The someone who loves you also has your back. Just curl up, snooze, and enjoy the fact that everything really is OK.

(And if it isn't, it could always be worse, you just need to use your imagination.)

72

You're never too old to play.

Seriously. There'll be days when the sun's out, it's warm on your back – and it feels good. It's then time to kick up your paws and cavort like a puppy. Who cares what everyone else thinks?

73

Wink at people. It confuses them.

After all, how are they going to *know* it's not a secret code?

74

Cold in bed?

Tuck your nose underneath your ankles and you'll warm up in a jiffy! *

(*May need a modicum of practice.)

75

Show your appreciation for a well-prepared meal.

So what if you just burped? Your host should be grateful you so clearly enjoyed your meal. Burp and move on.

76

Every day is a new day.

Start afresh every day. Widdling on the floor or chewing the remote doesn't count on day 2. Enjoy a new start.

77

Be a fair weather hound.

If it's cold outside, it's OK to wimp out. There's a certain level of comfort that one can cope without. However, there *is* a comfort threshold – and this must never be passed.

78

Trot, don't walk.

Why? Because it looks goooood. Show that figure of yours to its best advantage. People won't be able to help but look. And admire.

79

Read the situation.

That place by the fire? If anyone wanted it, they'd be straight in. They're not, so move on in! Take the opportunity.

80

Get your beauty sleep.

Is there a connection between a greyhound's superior good looks and their penchant for sleeping? Probably! They're equally good at sleeping and being enchantingly good-looking.

81

Wag appropriately.

If someone's a bit stingy with the treat, a half-hearted tail wag might be just the snub needed to encourage them to pull their socks up.

82

If it hasn't got an incentive, don't bother.

A ball with no treats in? What kind of a toy is that? That's right – it's no toy at all. It's OK to ask 'what's in it for me?'

83

Don't lose your bounce.

There's lots to be happy about. Cheese! Broccoli! Biscuits!

Life is good – enjoy the edible things.

84

When it's time for food, it's not time for conversation.

Get your head right in there and enjoy all those flavours. Plenty of time for chit-chat later.

85

Run naked!

Obviously not literally. However, the principle stands. Be free. Be liberated. Be fantastic!

86

Eat your greens.

Is that a broccoli stem you have right there? I hope you're not going to throw it away...

87

Selective hearing is OK up to a point.

Only you can work out how much you're able to get away with.

Looking cute will buy you even more patience.

88

Fetch a stick? Really?

Seriously, some people will just do things for the sake of doing them.

There are better things to do. Like sleeping. And also hinting for treats.

89

Nudge!

Yep, that's right. A gentle nudge may be all the encouragement needed for someone just to move that little bit faster, give you what you want, or just to remind them that you're right here.

90

Boring conversation?

It happens to us all. We strike up a chat, and before we know it, we're in Boring Country, on the fast train to Snooze Land.

You're gifted if you can sleep with your eyes open, but if not, just a twitch of the ears every now and then saves the need for committing anything more to a dull conversation.

91

Sleeping with your eyes open doesn't really count.

Fall asleep frequently in meetings or at concerts? No problem! Practice sleeping with your eyes open – give the semblance of politeness, while catching up on some shut-eye (without the shut eyes!)

As an aside: In a church setting, if you mistakenly fall asleep with your eyes closed, you can rescue the situation by quietly murmuring 'Amen' before opening your eyes.

92

A well-timed sigh can do wonders.

Not getting enough attention? Need a bit of a fuss, or for someone to fetch you some cheese from the fridge?

Say no more. A sigh will provoke pity in the hardest heart.

Extra Mature Cheddar? Here we come!

93

Get a routine, and force everyone else in the household to adhere to it.

Why *wouldn't* you like a walk out for a wee at half past eleven at night?

94

Help others to eat their dinner.

If your pal is not eating quickly enough, just lean in to give moral support. Perhaps also breathe on them.

If they're unable or unwilling to finish, finders keepers!

95

Ditch the weather forecast.

You don't need it.

Tap in the downstairs loo dripping? That means it's cold enough for the hound to wear a coat.

Dog curled up into an impossibly small ball? That means it'll be chilly tonight – stick the heating on, and turn a blind eye to the hound's sleep location of choice.

96

Wondering how your hound is settling in?

Greyhounds sleep more and more upside down the more comfortable they get in their home. Apparently.

97

Use your hungry face.

Even if others tell you 'It's NOT time!' it could well be that dinner is overdue. Everyone knows there are five hound hours to every human one.

98

Respect the laminate.

Take extra care when cornering. Greyhounds have been known to faceplant the wall when taking a corner too wide, too fast, and too enthusiastically.

99

Never underestimate the power of eyeballing people.

You know you're sorted when you just have to look at your people a certain way, and they visibly melt. Job done – you're in there for keeps.

100

Enjoy the moment.

Take time to concentrate on the moment's pleasure – whether it's a long walk, or a long snooze.

101

Remember where you've
been, but don't forget
where you're going.

It's great to leave the training track behind. But
it's not for dwelling on – onward and upward!

102

Give the underdog a chance.

Greyhounds have a rough deal. Look out for the underdogs and cut them some slack. Rescue a dog rather than buying one from a puppy breeder. You'll be part of the solution, not part of the problem, by saving a life as well as not supporting the puppy industry. For every puppy bought from a breeder, there's one less opportunity for an unwanted to dog to find a home. Many greyhounds are 'disposed' of when they're no longer wanted for the track. There are already so many unwanted dogs in the world with no hope of a good life – give one a home and you'll be glad you did.

Thankyou

Thanks so much for reading this book. I hope you enjoyed it!

If you fancy investigating rescued greyhounds for yourself, there are some fantastic greyhound charities out there – Sean came from GRWE (Greyhound Rescue, West of England) but there are also many others.

You may like to read:

- *Retired Greyhounds: A Guide to Care and Understanding* by Carol Baby
- *Retired Racing Greyhounds For Dummies* by Lea Livingood
- Don't forget to check out other Greyhound books.

If you liked this book, please help others to find it by leaving a review on Amazon or GoodReads (or both!) My author page can be reached at

http://www.amazon.co.uk/Angela-Reed-Fox/e/B00RG5ECAQ/ref=sr_ntt_srch_lnk_1?qid=1435414471&sr=8-1

Also, do keep in touch on Facebook and Twitter – I'd like your feedback on what I'm doing next.

Printed in Great Britain
by Amazon

78349815R00078